Contents

The leading of Liverpool	4
Path to glory	6
The first title	10
New frontiers	16
Wembley wonders	24
The second title	28
A second great team	36
A new decade	42
The third title	50
Shankly's only book	56
The swansong	60
Man of the people	72
Family life	76
Off the field	78
OBE	81

Sport Media
A Trinity Mirror Business

Written by: Simon Hughes & William Hughes
Produced by: Glen Hind & Jamie Dunmore

Executive Editor: Ken Rogers
Senior Editor: Steve Hanrahan
Senior Art Editor: Rick Cooke
Senior Production Editor: Paul Dove

Writers: Chris McLoughlin, David Randles, Gavin Kirk, John Hynes, Alan Jewell
Design Team: Barry Parker, Colin Sumpter, Alison Gilliland, James Kenyon, Lisa Critchley

Photography: Trinity Mirror, PA Photos & Mirrorpix
Printed by William Gibbons

Sales & Marketing Manager:
Elizabeth Morgan 0151 285 8412
Write to: Sport Media, PO BOX 48, Liverpool L69 3EB

The leading of **Liverpool**

THERE was no great fanfare when Bill Shankly was appointed manager of Liverpool.

The 46-year-old Scot had done a steady if unspectacular job in charge of Carlisle United, Grimsby Town, Workington and Huddersfield Town and many saw him merely as the next man in charge of a club seemingly content to tread water.

Shankly soon identified that mindset and made it his business to change it. The Liverpool directors had overlooked Shankly before. He was interviewed for the post in 1951 following George Kay's resignation. However, he knew he would never be able to accept the job after being asked how he felt about the board's wish to scrutinise team selections. Later that decade, the directors quickly discovered that in their new manager they had an irresistible force determined to awake the club from their slumbers and lead them into a land of untold glories.

Before Shankly took over, Liverpool had won five major honours in the shape of the top-flight championships of 1901, 1906, 1922, 1923 and 1947. But in the twelve-and-a-half years since their last success, the club had dropped into the second tier of English football and seemed happy to accept their fate.

Few managers have so transformed a football club in the manner in which Shankly overhauled Liverpool. Few have possessed such a potent combination of passion, charisma and sheer force of personality. The psychology and the soundbites became part of his legend.

There were plenty of tears shed when he made his shock resignation from Anfield in the summer of 1974. The club he left was unrecognisable from the one he entered in December 1959. For a start Liverpool's list of major honours had more than doubled with the roll of silverware now including the FA Cup and a European title. More than that, he established a dynasty that would set the club on a path of success that would last another 16 years.

To mark the 50th anniversary of the Scot's arrival at Anfield, Fifty Years of Shankly, sets out to celebrate the man who introduced a winning mentality that has been synonymous with the Reds ever since.

Using rarely seen archive pictures, including many from the vaults of the Daily Mirror and the Liverpool Daily Post and Echo, this souvenir magazine focuses on Shankly and his unique bond with the Liverpool fans.

Beyond the trophies, Shankly's lasting legacy was his unbreakable bond with the club's supporters. A born socialist, he established Liverpool as the people's club long before the phrase rolled off the tongue of David Moyes. Famed for the way he would reply to fans' letters and requests, Shankly did everything within his power to make their dreams come true because he shared those same hopes and ambitions. At heart, he was one of them.

And he made those people happy.

THE LEADING OF LIVERPOOL

Shaking hands with chairman TV Williams after becoming manager of Liverpool Football Club in December 1959

Path to glory

BILL SHANKLY was appointed Liverpool manager on 1 December, 1959. The club was decaying in the Second Division following relegation six seasons earlier. Supporters were in dire need of inspiration.

The Liverpool Echo described Shankly as a 'bullet-headed Scot' adding: 'Whatever the future holds, it certainly won't be dull.' They were right.

Shankly agreed to become Reds boss after not receiving the financial backing of the board at previous club, Huddersfield Town. With future Manchester United legend Denis Law already in his squad, Shankly wanted to sign another two Scots to help his team challenge for promotion to the First Division. Those players were Ron Yeats and Ian St John.

Shankly later said, "Yeats and St. John were the players Huddersfield needed, but they couldn't afford to buy them."

When Phil Taylor resigned as manager, Liverpool chairman TV Williams approached Shankly. "How would you like to manage the best club in the country?" Williams asked. "Is Matt Busby packing up?" Shankly responded with typical humour before quickly agreeing a move to Anfield with an annual salary of £2500. Ironically, his last game in charge of Huddersfield was a 1-0 win against Liverpool.

Upon his appointment, Shankly declared: "I am very pleased to have been chosen as manager of Liverpool Football Club – a club with so much great potential. It is my opinion that Liverpool have a crowd of followers which ranks among the greatest in the game. They deserve success – and I hope to be able to do something toward helping them achieve it. I make no promises except that I shall put everything I have into the job I have so willingly undertaken."

After losing 4-0 at home to Cardiff City in his first match in charge, Shankly understood that there would be no short-term fixes to Liverpool's problems and soon set about re-shaping his squad with the primary aim of achieving promotion. He also faced problems off the field. "…when I arrived at Anfield, it was the biggest slum in Liverpool," he said. "…we had to bring in water from Oakfield Road at a cost of £3000 to flush the toilets and the ground was dilapidated."

Liverpool finished third for two seasons on the run. Then, by the summer of 1961, Shankly was ready to make the two signings that would shape the club's success over the next decade. He told the Liverpool board that his side would reach the First Division if he was allowed to buy the players that he wanted to sign three years earlier for Huddersfield, Yeats and St John.

The board's answer was emphatic, "We can't afford them." Luckily for Liverpool, there was one director who shared Shankly's vision. He retorted, "We cannot afford not to sign them."

St John quickly developed an understanding with strike partner Roger Hunt with the pair scoring 64 league goals between them the following campaign. Yeats was appointed captain and immediately became an integral part of the team's spine.

Together, they helped Liverpool to promotion in their debut season, finishing eight points clear of Leyton Orient and ending eight years in the Second Division wilderness.

1962 was crowned as memorable year for the Shankly family with Bob Shankly, Bill's brother, guiding Dundee to their first ever First Division title in Scotland, finishing ahead of Rangers and Celtic.

Liverpool celebrate winning promotion back to Division One in April 1962

PATH TO GLORY

Enjoying afternoon tea in the lounge of a Blackpool hotel in 1961, Shankly is joined by chairman TV Williams, director Harry Latham and players Jim Harrower and Bert Slater

Mr. Shankly Arrives At Anfield

Mr. Bill Shankly, the new manager of Liverpool F.C., took over officially at Anfield today, although he was at the ground on Saturday to watch the reserves play. Left to right in the round table conference this afternoon are: Bob Paisley, first team trainer, Mr. Shankly, Mr. T. V. Williams, chairman, and Reuben Bennett, the chief coach.

THE FIRST TITLE

Shankly and his team celebrate at Anfield after winning the Division One championship in 1964

Shankly's success story gathered pace in the mid-1960s as the Reds began to establish themselves as a force at home and abroad

The first title

LIVERPOOL consolidated their position during their first season back in the First Division, finishing eighth.

Shankly's side reached the FA Cup semi-final but missed out on a trip to Wembley by losing 1-0 to Leicester City. Such setbacks would later inspire Shankly to greatness.

1962/63 also brought Shankly his first experience of the Merseyside derby, with both games ending draws in a season where the Blues finished as champions.

It quickly became apparent to Shankly that the rivalry between Liverpool and Everton was like no other. It prompted him to commend the people of the city.

"If I had a business and I needed a workforce to be successful I would take my workforce from Merseyside," he said. "And we would wipe the floor with everybody. They've got hearts of gold…and they can work. All they need is to be handled like human beings, not bullied and pushed around.

"So I'd pick my workforce from Merseyside and anybody else can pick theirs from anywhere else and we'd have a go with them. And I'd win. We'd be successful.

"Merseyside is a distressed area with a lot of unemployment. People have a hard time. But they've got a big spirit. I think deep down they've got a spirit that when they're on your side and all working together they take a bit of beating."

Shankly added Willie Stevenson (Rangers) and Peter Thompson (Preston) to his squad ahead of the 1963/64 season. Three defeats in their first three home games gave no inclination of the campaign ahead as the Reds charged to the title with three games to spare, clinching it at Anfield with a 5-0 win over Arsenal. Liverpool were now officially the best team in the country for the first time since 1947.

Once again, Ian St John and Roger Hunt were instrumental in the campaign and together with Alf Arrowsmith, they contributed 67 of the Reds' 97 league goals. With young Scottish goalkeeper, Tommy Lawrence, fully established after promotion from the reserves, Shankly had created a spine to his team that would remain immovable for the years that followed.

Ian Callaghan opens the scoring against Manchester United in April 1964

At a board meeting in 1964. Pictured from left are: SC Reakes, CJ Hill, H Cartwright, GA Richards, RL Martindale, TV Williams (chairman), JS McInnes (secretary), Shankly, EAF Sawyer and HK Latham

50 YEARS OF SHANKLY

Toasting the 1964 Division One title after a 5-0 win over Arsenal

The 1964 champions pose with the Division One trophy. They are, back row, from left: Gordon Milne, Gerry Byrne, Tommy Lawrence, Ronnie Moran, Willie Stevenson, Bob Paisley (trainer). Front row: Reuben Bennett (trainer), Ian Callaghan, Roger Hunt, Ian St John, TV Williams (chairman), Ron Yeats, Alf Arrowsmith, Peter Thompson and Shankly

THE FIRST TITLE

Shankly became known for finding time to reply to letters and requests from Liverpool supporters. This played a part in helping him establish a unique bond with the club's fans

NEW FRONTIERS

Shankly and his squad cross the road near the Oatlands Park Hotel, Weybridge for a light training session ahead of the 1965 FA Cup final

New frontiers

IN THE 45-years since their first European tie, Liverpool have faced all of the continent's most decorated clubs. It all started, though, in Iceland against Reykjavik.

"Entering Europe was something new for us and you encounter different things...different climates, languages, food," Shankly said. "And it takes a long time to get yourself stabilised in Europe. The Europeans are devious. They tell you, 'Liverpool are too good, too strong…' And this is to soften you up and simmer you down to try and beat you."

KR Reykjavik were easy opponents, with Liverpool winning 5-0 in Iceland and 6-1 at Anfield. By now, Shankly had a clear identity with the Kop,

"Football, above all, is a working class game and the Kop is a special place. One Saturday at twenty-five past two I went onto the Kop. And a little bloke said to me: 'Stand here Bill. You'll get a better view.'

"At the end of the day the game belongs to the people. And if you don't have the people on your side then you've got nothing. I was a working class boy. I was one of them. I wouldn't let anybody say anything against the Kop."

Shankly's allegiance with supporters was evident during the second leg against Reykjavik when, sympathising with Liverpool's hapless opponents, the Kop demanded that the Reds allow the Icelanders to score. Shankly agreed and the tie finished 11-1 on aggregate.

In the second round, Liverpool were paired with Anderlecht whose team featured seven players from the Belgian national side that had recently forced a 2-2 draw with England, impressing Shankly.

Ahead of the game, Shankly decided that Liverpool would play in an all-red strip for the first time, a plan he later discussed with wife, Nessie.

"The introduction of the all scarlet strip had a huge psychological effect. I went home that night and said to Ness, 'You know something...tonight I went out onto Anfield and for the first time there was a glow like a fire was burning.'"

Anderlecht wilted in the red-hot Anfield atmosphere with Liverpool winning 3-0, goals arriving from St John, Hunt and Yeats. A narrow second leg victory in Brussels secured a tie with Cologne in the next round.

Two goalless draws forced a replay held in neutral Rotterdam where it finished 2-2. With the penalty shoot-out yet to be recognised by UEFA, Liverpool progressed to the semi-final at the toss of a coin, much to the relief of Ron Yeats who had lost the toss at kick-off and the start of extra-time.

Against Inter Milan in the first leg of the semi, gates were locked at Anfield hours before the kick-off, prompting captain Yeats to question where all the fans had gone as the team bus drew towards the stadium. "They're already in the ground…it's a 54,000 capacity sell out."

Liverpool had already won the FA Cup days before (see page 24) and the success created a frenzied atmosphere inside Anfield. With Italian greats Giacinto Facchetti and Sandro Mazzola in their side as well as Spanish pair Luis Suarez and Joaquin, Inter were holders of the European Cup.

Ahead of the kick-off, Shankly sent Gerry Byrne and Gordon Milne out onto the pitch with the FA Cup to stir the crowd even further and it worked with Roger Hunt handing the Reds a fourth minute lead. Mazzola equalised but strikes from Ian Callaghan and Ian St John secured a 3-1 win.

A week later, during the return leg in Italy, Liverpool played in front of 90,000 fans. Ahead of the match, an off the field PR campaign had been waged against Liverpool players by the Italian press. Then on the pitch, Inter were recipients of some generous and unusual decisions by the referee who was later found to be corrupt. The hosts won 3-0 and progressed to the final where they defeated Benfica, 1-0.

"I was told before the game in Milan that whatever happened we would not go through to the final," Shankly later said.

Despite the huge disappointment in missing out on a final in their first season competing in Europe, Shankly also believed the setback would help Liverpool in years to come.

"We learned about travel, the waiting around and all the little things that can go wrong like bad roads and poor training pitches. These were lessons absorbed by the club which later helped Liverpool win things in Europe."

Shankly is presented with his tie pin and cuff links set by the chairman of the 'Wonderful Whackers' club Ted Black watched by some members of his squad

NEW FRONTIERS

Boarding planes to Europe became a regular experience for Shankly and his squad. Here, they head to Belgium for a Cup Winners' Cup tie against Anderlecht in December 1965

50 YEARS OF SHANKLY
SOUVENIRS OF A LEGEND

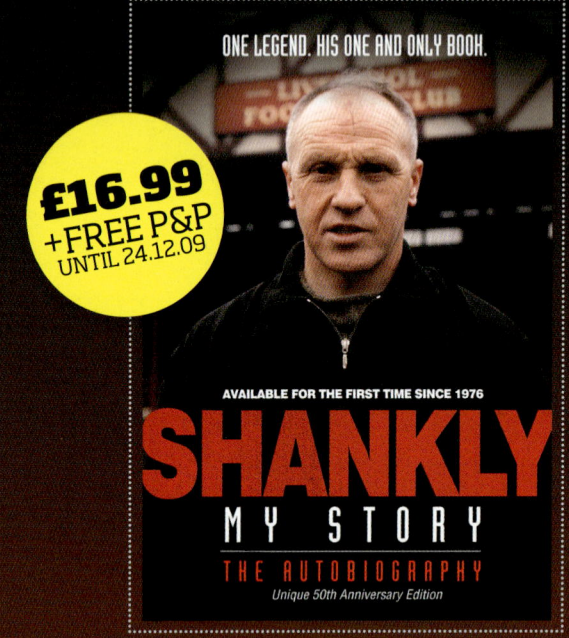

£16.99 + FREE P&P UNTIL 24.12.09

One legend. His one and only book. Available for the first time since 1976

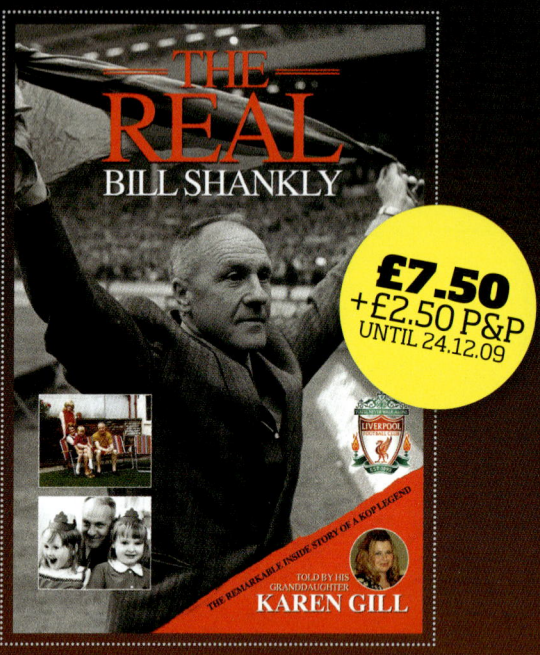

£7.50 + £2.50 P&P UNTIL 24.12.09

The remarkable inside story as told by his granddaughter Karen Gill. Includes family pics

FROM £99.99

Bill Shankly bronze statue, by respected sculptor Tom Murphy

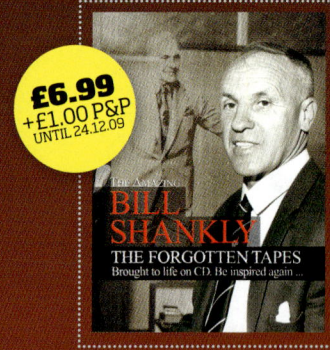

£6.99 + £1.00 P&P UNTIL 24.12.09

Lost interviews brought to life on CD. Hear the man himself and be inspired again

£14.99 + FREE P&P UNTIL 24.12.09

Stories behind the signings that shaped football history

PLUS... LIMITED EDITION PRINTS, CALENDAR AND LIFESIZE BUST

TO ORDER CALL 0845 143 0001
OR LOG ON TO WWW.MERSEYSHOP.COM

NEW FRONTIERS

Talking to children who took part in a game of street football. Shankly had watched the game from a flat above Eldon Grove, off Scotland Road

Enjoying a cup of tea with the children who played in the street football match in August 1965

Top: Conducting a training session in July 1965

Left: In conversation with Bob Paisley and Joe Fagan at Melwood

NEW FRONTIERS

Taking part in one of his favourite five-a-sides

Wembley wonders

WEST BROMWICH ALBION, Stockport County, Leicester City and Chelsea were all beaten on the run to Liverpool's first FA Cup final in their 73-year history.

Goals from Willie Stevenson and Peter Thompson against Chelsea in the semi at Villa Park, which was played only three days after the Reds' replayed European Cup match against Cologne, set up a trip to Wembley to face Don Revie's Leeds United.

"Tension's a big thing," Shankly reflected. "Liverpool had never won the Cup and neither had Leeds. We were coming out of the tunnel and I was alongside Leeds manager Don Revie. I turned around and said to Bobby Collins, the Leeds captain: 'How are you Bobby?' He said: 'I feel awful.'"

Liverpool had won the League title the season before but what fans wanted most was the FA Cup. A goalless ninety minutes did little to alleviate the nerves as the game spiralled towards a replay. What most observers didn't realise was that full-back Gerry Byrne had played virtually the whole game with a broken collarbone following a collision with opposing skipper Collins in the fourth minute.

With no substitutes permitted, Byrne played the whole game, including extra-time with nobody outside the Liverpool dressing room aware as to the extent of his injury.

Three minutes into extra time, Liverpool took the lead through Roger Hunt but Billy Bremner equalised before the half was out. It took until five minutes before the end for the game to be decided when Ian St John connected with Ian Callaghan's cross to hand Liverpool and Shankly the trophy.

"Grown men were crying and it was the greatest feeling any human being could have to see what we had done," Shankly said. "There have been many proud moments. Wonderful, fantastic moments. But that was the greatest day, the one I treasure the most."

Ian St John heads the goal that gave Liverpool their first FA Cup win

WEMBLEY WONDERS

Captain Ron Yeats and team-mates celebrate

WEMBLEY WONDERS

Left: Shankly and his captain Ron Yeats delight in the moment of triumph soon after the final whistle at Wembley in 1965

Below: Making a speech with his FA Cup final winners during a reception at the Liverpool Empire

Shankly with his bread and butter, the Football League championship, and other trophies including the FA Charity Shield

THE SECOND TITLE

The **second** title

BILL SHANKLY chose only 14 players during the campaign en-route to the title in 1966. It was the fewest number any manager in the football league had used before achieving the same feat.

Consistency in team selection became Liverpool's strength and it was marked by the fact that beyond the usual match-day 12, Alf Arrowsmith made only five appearances while Bobby Graham played once.

The Reds lost seven times but were ruthless in front of goal, especially at Anfield. Roger Hunt scored 30 times in the league, his best tally for Liverpool in the First Division.

Shankly had now made his own indelible mark on Liverpool. "When I go to see a team I want to be able to identify them," he said. "I want to be able to say: 'They can play. They've got a system.' And that's what Liverpool had. A system that could be identified.

"Tommy Docherty had it. I could tell a Chelsea player from his panache, his control and his kicking of the ball. I say to myself: 'That's a Tommy Docherty player' because he'd given them a bit of style and class. I'm looking for a team to be identifiable, to know what they're doing, what each other's doing and what they should be doing. This is what football is all about. It's a really simple game."

The Reds' on-pitch understanding was exemplified with West Ham, Everton, Northampton and Blackburn being victims of five goal hammerings while Nottingham Forest, Arsenal, Sunderland and Blackpool all conceded four at Anfield.

The title was secured with a game to spare, with both goals predictably coming from Hunt in a 2-1 win over Chelsea at Anfield.

A week later, Liverpool had the opportunity to make it a league and cup double when they travelled to Hampden Park to face Borussia Dortmund in the final of the Cup Winners Cup. Juventus, Standard Liege and Honved were beaten before the Reds drew Celtic in the semi-final. Despite losing 1-0 in the first leg at Parkhead, strikes from Tommy Smith and Geoff Strong in the Anfield return eased the path to Glasgow.

Despite another goal from Hunt, Shankly and Liverpool learnt another harsh lesson in European football with an unfortunate own goal from Ron Yeats contributing towards a 2-1 defeat.

The following season, Liverpool competed in the European Cup for a second time, experiencing an even bigger lesson than two years earlier against Inter Milan.

After knocking out Romanian champions Petrolul Ploiesti in the first round in a replay played at Heysel, Shankly's side drew Dutch side, Ajax. A 5-1 defeat at a fog-bound De Meer meant the end of Liverpool's European odyssey for the Sixties.

"We got beaten and it was mainly through haphazard play," Shankly said. "Although in the tiny parts of the game that I saw, they were better than us."

Chris Lawler's 90th minute consolation gave the Reds the faintest hope for the return at Anfield a week later, but Ajax, buoyed by Johan Cruyff forced a 2-2 draw.

Liverpool put Sunderland on the back foot at Roker Park during the title-winning season of 1965/66

THE SECOND TITLE

Shankly raises a smile as he parades the club's trophies in August 1966

50 YEARS OF SHANKLY

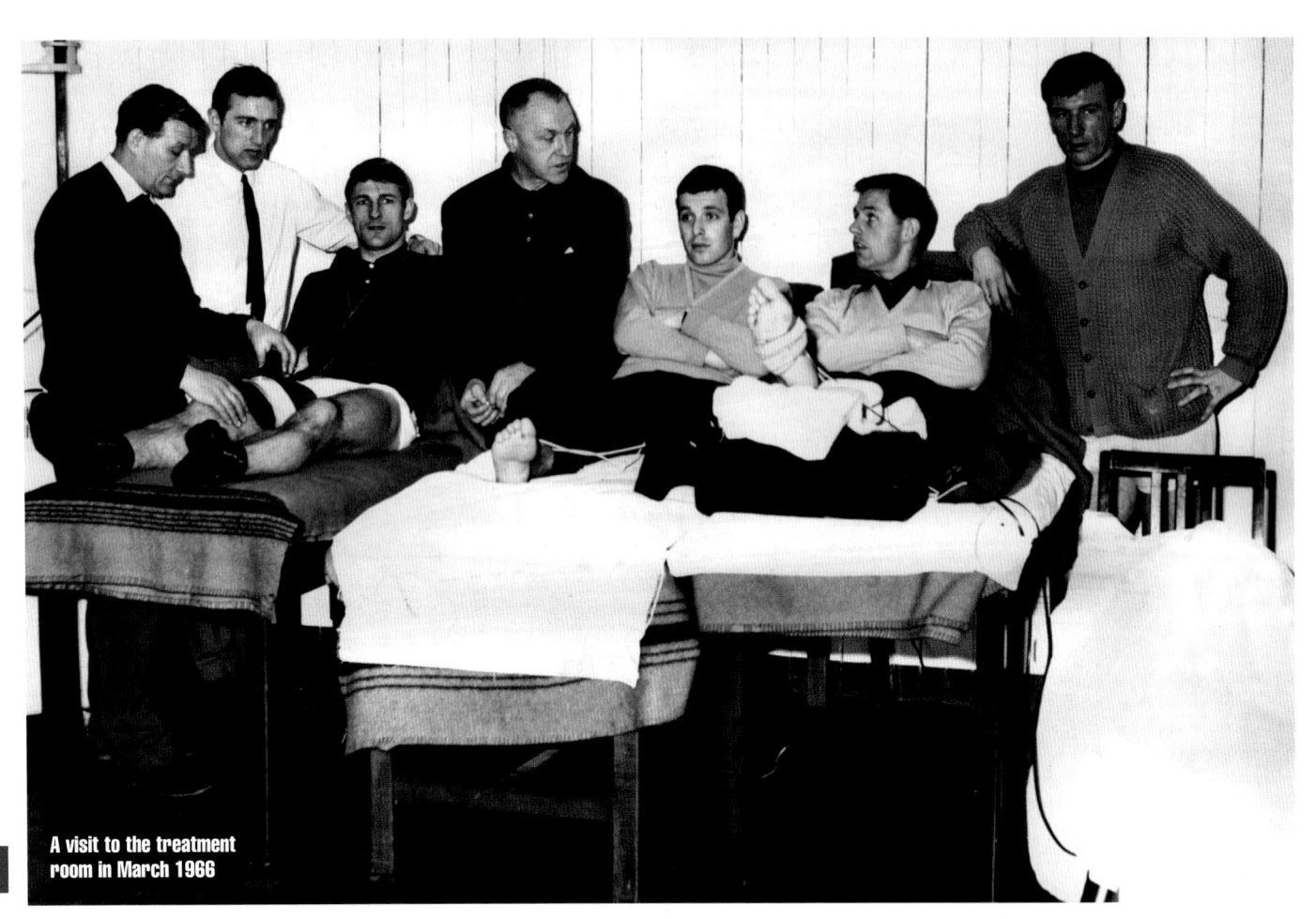

A visit to the treatment room in March 1966

Baby Paula O'Sullivan in the arms of Reds captain Ron Yeats. She was named after the entire 1965 FA Cup-winning team plus Shankly and his two asistants

THE SECOND TITLE

Above: Liverpool Exchange MP Bessie Braddock presents Bill Shankly and Celtic's Jock Stein with cheques at the 1966 Manager of the Year awards at the Cafe Royal

Left: Passing on some tips to young players during a training session

Roger Hunt scores Liverpool's equaliser in the 1966 European Cup Winners' Cup final against Borussia Dortmund at Hampden Park

Ron Yeats kicks out in frustration after scoring the extra-time own goal that won Borussia Dortmund the 1966 European Cup Winners' Cup

THE SECOND TITLE

Chatting to chairman TV Williams and head groundsman Arthur Riley after the referee called off a match in November 1966

Being greeted by Celtic manager Jock Stein after Liverpool's plane landed at Renfrew Airport the day before the first leg of the clubs' European Cup Winners' Cup semi-final at Parkhead in April 1966

A SECOND GREAT TEAM

A pensive Shankly wears an expression of concern as his Liverpool team struggle to match the peaks of previous seasons

Opposite: Shankly scratches his head
during a pre-season photo-shoot

A **second** great team

Top: Signing Emlyn Hughes in February 1967
Below: On board a plane to Lisbon in November 1969

FOLLOWING the highs of the mid-1960s, Shankly slowly saw his side's powers wane as the decade came to a close.

Liverpool had enjoyed a rich vein of success as they won the league in 1964, the FA Cup in 1965 and the league again in 1966. They had also narrowly missed out on European glory in 1965 and 1966, reaching the semi-final of the European Cup and the final of the European Cup Winners' Cup respectively.

In the years that followed, Shankly stayed loyal to the majority of the players who had helped him achieve those successes. Yet although they came close on a couple of occasions, Liverpool were unable to regain the league title.

In 1967 they finished fifth, nine points adrift of champions Manchester United; in 1968 they were third; a year later they finished as runners-up but in 1969/70 the Reds ended the season 15 points behind champions Everton.

The Liverpool manager later admitted that he had persisted with some of the players too long. He held firm to the belief that they were still of the right age to perform but perhaps the extra demands of European football had left some of them weary.

That 1969/70 campaign also saw Liverpool's FA Cup ambitions disappear with defeat at Second Division strugglers Watford. It was a result that finally helped Shankly accept that he needed to re-model the team if the Reds were to repeat the heights of their earlier glory days.

For the first time, he began to see that the hunger he instilled in every man to wear the Liverbird upon his chest had started to evaporate from a few of his men.

"The changeover wasn't easy because it meant losing men who had been great servants, who had won the FA Cup for Liverpool for the first time and put them on the map. But the changes had to be made."

It was little wonder that Shankly had felt such a strong sense of loyalty to his players. After all, they were the ones who had enabled him to help Liverpool to a string of successes. Those players were idolised by the Liverpool fans who turned up to watch them and came up with chants in salute to their heroes.

Shankly was therefore reluctant to break up his squad. But following that setback at Vicarage Road, he acknowledged that he needed to shake things up. There could be no room for sentiment.

Out went established stars from that first team like Ron Yeats, Tommy Lawrence, Roger Hunt and Gerry Byrne, to be replaced by a new wave of players such as Ray Clemence, Steve Heighway and Brian Hall - all charged with restoring Liverpool to the top table of football at home and abroad.

50 YEARS OF SHANKLY

A SECOND GREAT TEAM

Holding court during a chat with the Press and, inset, watching a youth team game between Liverpool and Tranmere at Anfield in December 1969

41

50 YEARS OF SHANKLY

Shankly makes a point during a team-talk as Larry Lloyd listens in

A NEW DECADE

43

50 YEARS OF SHANKLY

Chatting to Tom Finney, the player he admired above all others

Shankly with his bootroom boys: Bob Paisley, Joe Fagan, Ronnie Moran, Reuben Bennett and Tom Saunders

A new decade

WITH Shankly settled on the need to revamp his squad, the Scot set about the business of building his second great Liverpool team.

Youngsters such as Steve Heighway, Brian Hall, John McLaughlin and Larry Lloyd were gradually integrated into the side, while John Toshack was signed from Cardiff City to give added physical presence in attack.

The Reds also had a new captain with homegrown talent Tommy Smith taking over the armband from Ron Yeats.

There was an inevitable bedding-in process and the team again finished off the pace in the league in 1970/71, 14 points behind champions Arsenal.

However, they gave a glimpse of their potential in a thrilling FA Cup run that saw them defeat neighbours Everton in the last four to earn a Wembley date with Arsenal in the final.

There was plenty to cheer about when Steve Heighway put the Reds ahead in extra-time But it proved to be a false dawn, as goals from George Graham and Charlie George gave the Gunners the double.

Even so, Shankly's side had served notice of what the 'new' Liverpool might achieve and, in the week leading up to the final, the Reds boss had conducted another astute piece of business.

Kevin Keegan, a young striker, had been signed from Scunthorpe United and travelled to Wembley with the squad to watch the final. He made such an impression in pre-season that Shankly put him straight into the team for the first game of the 1971/72 campaign. He would go on to form such a good understanding with Toshack that a television show conducted an experiment to see if they were telepathic.

While on the pitch matters were always Shankly's primary concern, he also prided himself with the way Anfield had been transformed during his tenure.

He had described the club's ground as an eyesore when he took charge in 1959 but with the opening of the new Main Stand in the early 1970s, he now declared Anfield fit for a king.

The 1971/72 season saw Liverpool show they were real title contenders again as they played their part in one of the most exciting title races on record.

Along with Manchester City, Leeds United and Derby County, the Reds were in the hunt for the title until the final game. In the final analysis they finished third behind champions Derby and Leeds. Only a single point separated all four teams.

It provided further evidence that Shankly's Liverpool were once again ready to challenge on all fronts.

Passing on some information to John Toshack in training

50 YEARS OF SHANKLY

Top: Posing for a team photo in the car park in January 1971. The team is, from left, back row: Peter Thompson, Alec Lindsay, Ray Clemence, Tommy Lawrence, Chris Lawler, Ian Ross.
Middle: Alun Evans, John McLaughlin, Larry Lloyd, John Toshack, Steve Heighway, Phil Boersma, Brian Hall.
Front: Bobby Graham, Emlyn Hughes, Ron Yeats, Shankly, Tommy Smith, Ian Callaghan and Bob Paisley

Left: Leading his men out for the 1971 FA Cup final against Arsenal

A NEW DECADE

With Manchester City manager Joe Mercer in the Maine Road tunnel ahead of the teams' clash in 1971

Enjoying a laugh as Jimmy Hill emerges from the tunnel at Highbury to take over as an emergency linesman in September 1972

With new signing Kevin Keegan in May 1971. It would prove a shrewd acquisition

A NEW DECADE

Shankly at the breakfast table

50 YEARS OF SHANKLY

50

THE THIRD TITLE

A proud Shankly lifts the Football League championship aloft in 1973, while joyous Liverpool fans celebrate the title triumph

The **third** title

THE disappointment of missing out on the title in 1971/72 only fuelled the desire within the Liverpool squad.

Nottingham Forest midfielder Peter Cormack was the only major addition to the squad during the summer and the Reds made a good start with 2-0 home wins against both Manchester sides in their opening two games.

With the team losing just once at Anfield, Liverpool were consistent throughout the season. Part of the secret was that Shankly preferred consistency of selection with only 16 players used during the whole league campaign.

Arsenal mounted a strong challenge to Liverpool's quest for the title but with the forward partnership of Kevin Keegan and John Toshack continuing to flourish, the Reds ran out winners by three points.

Shankly's men were not content with the bread and butter of the league however and wanted dessert in the shape of the UEFA Cup.

Having overcome Frankfurt, AEK Athens, Dynamo Berlin, Dynamo Dresden and Tottenham, Liverpool were looking forward to meeting German side Borussia Monchengladbach in the final.

The Reds stood on the precipice of creating club history. For the first time since their formation, Liverpool were within reach of winning two major trophies in the same season.

They had unfinished business in Europe with the memories of the heartaches of Inter Milan in 1965 and Borussia Dortmund the following season still relatively fresh in the memory.

Shankly's men swept into a 3-0 lead at Anfield but Ray Clemence also saved a penalty from Jupp Heynckes which would have a greater bearing on the outcome than people perhaps realised at the time.

Monchengladbach won the return leg 2-0 and, but for Clemence's save from the spot at Anfield, would have lifted the trophy on the away goals' rule.

As it was, Liverpool triumphed 3-2 on aggregate to lift their first European trophy and achieve the unique feat of major honours at home and abroad in the same campaign.

It proved beyond doubt that Liverpool were back at the peak of their powers and their achievements filled Shankly with pride.

He later declared it his greatest season as he reflected on the achievement of building a new team that had not only matched the glories of his first great side but surpassed them.

What was more, Liverpool had achieved what they had with a young team that was clearly capable of achieving much more.

Shankly's appetite was far from satisfied. At the start of the following season, he is reported to have gathered the players together in the dressing room and told them: "Thanks for last year boys. Your medals are in a box over there. Now forget it, we start at the bottom again."

Re-united with the League Championship again, left, and getting his hands on the UEFA Cup, above.

THE THIRD TITLE

Showing off the Bell's Manager of the Year award in 1973

Above: A hug from Emlyn Hughes

Right: Saluting the Kop with a helping hand from goalkeeping great Gordon Banks

THE THIRD TITLE

A red-shirted Shankly acknowledges the Kop as Leicester City players salute Liverpool as champions in April 1973

Shankly makes his way on ot the pitch to receive the Bell's Manager of the Year award before the home game against Chelsea in September 1973

55

50 YEARS OF SHANKLY

Shankly's only **book**

In 1976, Bill Shankly's only autobiography went on sale. At the time, someone at Liverpool Football Club decided it was too hot to handle, owing to some of its candid revelations, and banned it from being sold in the official club shop. Now re-published as part of the celebrations to mark the 50th anniversary of Shankly's arrival at Anfield, this exclusive extract reveals his proudest moment as Liverpool manager

'MY biggest thrill as a player was winning the FA Cup with Preston. My greatest day in football was when Liverpool won the FA Cup for the first time. But winning the League Championship for the third time, and with a brand new team, possibly gave me more satisfaction than anything. By achieving that, Liverpool equalled Arsenal's record of eight championships – and that same season, 1972/73, we brought home a European trophy, the UEFA Cup.

The policy of the new team was the same as that of the old. We played to our strengths. We pressurised everybody and made them run. We didn't concede many goals and perhaps we didn't score as many goals as we should have done, because we had the opposition back defending and blocking up their goal. The more players there are in the penalty box – even your own players – the more difficult it can be to score goals.

We had devised a system of play, which minimised the risk of injuries. The team played in sections of the field, like a relay. We didn't want players running the length of the field, stretching themselves unnecessarily, so our back men played in one area, and then passed on to the midfield men, in their area, and so on to the front men. So, whilst there was always room for individuals within our system, the work was shared out. It was no accident that during my time at Anfield eight players played more than three hundred league matches – Ian Callaghan 502, Chris Lawler 396, Roger Hunt 384, Peter Thompson 377, Tommy Lawrence 305. Emlyn Hughes, who had played 264 League matches during my time, later went well past the 300 mark and Ray Clemence, Kevin Keegan and Steve Heighway are among those well on the way at the time of writing.

We didn't believe in resting players simply because we had a heavy programme of matches. We wouldn't put in young players who were not familiar with the pattern and who would consequentially put extra pressure on the rest of the team.

Tony Waiters had joined our training staff for a while, and Tony is a very clever fellow. The initial training before one season, with Tony's ideas combining with ours, was tremendous. There was so much variation that the time passed quickly, and I have never known so much enjoyment at training. Tony had been all for signing Steve Heighway, and he saw Steve play more than anyone else on our staff. We picked up a few things from Tony and he possibly picked up a few ideas from us. He left us to play in goal for Burnley for a spell and later became manager of Plymouth.

I saw the emotion in players like Kevin Keegan and Emlyn Hughes when they were in tears after we got pipped for the League in 1971/72, Kevin's first season. We lost the League by a point. At Derby, when we were losing 1-0, Kevin was definitely obstructed in the box when their goalkeeper came and 'did' him, but no penalty was given. That would have won the League for us. Sam Longson, the Derby chairman, was at our last game at Arsenal, when we were robbed of a goal. Kevin went through and gave a slanted pass to John Toshack, who rammed the ball into the net. Everybody in the ground thought it was a goal, but is was disallowed for offside. So we finished third, behind Leeds on goal average, to Derby – who were away at some holiday camp abroad. I took encouragement from the fact that we had played so well at Highbury. The new team had emerged, and the following season we won the League with sixty points.

We were still strong on psychology of course. We even had a plaque put over the tunnel that takes the players from the dressing rooms to the pitch. Our maintenance foreman, Bert Johnson, had it painted, white letters on a red background: THIS IS ANFIELD. A form of intimidation.

Newcastle United came one day and their players were in good spirits. I couldn't understand it, because they never won any games at our ground. Joe Harvey was at the top of the steps leading down to the tunnel and the players were making their way out: John Tudor, Bob Moncur, and the rest. As Malcolm Macdonald came alongside Joe, he pointed at the plaque and said, "Joe, we are in the right ground."

I said, "You'll soon bloody find out you're in the right ground, son!" – only the words were stronger than that.

We beat Newcastle 5-0 that day – and they had never played better. They were the unluckiest team in the world. It could have been five goals each. It was a fantastic game. We played well and they played well, but we got the breaks and they got nothing. Ray Clemence was absolutely brilliant.

Kevin Keegan shoots towards goal in Liverpool's 3-0 FA Cup Final victory over Newcastle United. It would be Shankly's last competitive match in charge

Malcolm Macdonald took it very well. He was quoted in the papers as saying how quickly I had replied to what he had said before the game. Malcolm is a likeable chap and I'd have him in my team. He scores goals because he's unafraid and wants chances.

I always liked to see the opposition players when they walked into the ground and down to the dressing rooms. I would look up the Rothmans book or the News of the World football annual to refresh my mind on their first names, though I knew most of them of course. I would be ready for them when they arrived. I'd say things like, "Hello, Jimmy, it's a bit heavy, but it's not a bad ground. In actual fact, it's the kind of ground that suits us. We like to play in certain conditions and today's conditions are just what we wanted. Our players are just geared for it."

If it was heavy, if it was dry, if it was frosty – it made no difference. I'd say, "Just a touch of frost. I remember the last time we played on a frosty pitch – oh, we didn't half play well!"

Then I would go into our dressing room and say, "Christ, I've seen them coming in, boys. They've been out on the tiles! Bobby Moore looks older than me! I'm not joking, it's bloody unbelievable to see this. I'll tell you something – they were frightened to death!" I said this about everybody. If it had been Real Madrid I would have said the same.

Ron Greenwood and Bobby Moore were once quoted by a newspaper as saying how difficult it was for some teams to score against West Ham. They mentioned Liverpool as being one of them. Well, we went to play at West Ham the Monday after the start of a season and, about ten minutes into the second half, we scored our fifth goal. I turned to Greenwood and said, "I'll tell you something, Ron, we've got a chance of winning this game!"

We laid down our plans at the start of the season, the way Tottenham did when they won the double in 1960/61. They had one tactical talk at the beginning of the season, with Danny Blanchflower, John White, Bobby Smith, and all of them, and they didn't need any more talks. If you have a good team, a tactical talk at the start, sorting out all the basics so that you know what you are going to do, is enough – unless your players have bad memories. If things were not going right, I would say to the players, "We'll need to have another tactical talk – your bloody memories have gone! We had one three years ago, and we'll have to have another one!"

The players would usually be in the dressing room at about two o'clock for a Saturday game. Maybe one or two would leave it a bit later. When I was a player, I used to get ready about fifty minutes before a game. I used to take all day, taking off my clothes and putting on my football jersey

Above: Shankly's players read about him in the press

Right: Ray Clemence in action during the 1971 FA Cup final defeat to Arsenal

SHANKLY'S ONLY BOOK

Keegan under the watchful eye of Ron Greenwood, Shankly's old adversary, during England training.

shorts, socks and boots. Then I would sit and relax. If anyone said, "There's somebody outside looking for you", I would say, "I'll see them after the match." I wasn't bothered about handing out tickets and things like that. When I was in the dressing room I was finished with everything except the match. If somebody had said, "Your brother's outside", I would have said, "Well, tell him I'll see him next summer." I would rub myself down and put the bandages on my ankles and take my time.

The Liverpool players would probably chat for a few minutes and start getting ready about forty-five minutes before the game. I hated to see teams rushing at the last minute. That's rubbish. They should be ready in time, so they can relax. A lot of teams do things a certain way because they are superstitious and always have to rush to do something before they go out. I used to say, "Well, you are better doing it now than on the field!"

I would patter on about the opposition. I'd say, "Christ, I've seen that new boy of theirs and I'll tell you something now – he didn't sleep a wink last night! What's more, if you run him around he won't sleep a wink tonight either!"

At Preston I was brought up with a lot of funny fellows, and I was a funny fellow too. The trainer used to get us to start a laugh. We used to tell jokes about the old days, when they played in big boots and long drawers and had drooping moustaches. To have somebody in the dressing room who can crack jokes before the game is very good.

"I've seen their substitute," I'd tell our players at Liverpool, "and I hope to Christ he has to go on, because I'm bloody sure he doesn't want to go on!" This would be the banter, and I would encourage players to talk to one another. Some were very quiet, of course. Ian Callaghan would sit and say very little, but that didn't stop him from being the hardest-working player on the field.

I made it my business to know all about my players. I even knew the colour of their eyes. And I always had a high regard for Ian. One day a man came to see me and asked me if I could recommend one of my players who might be the type to join him in an insurance business, with a view to eventually becoming a partner. Without hesitation I told him, "Ian Callaghan's your man." Ian went into insurance and made a success of it. I could never have recommended the boy too highly.'

ONE LEGEND. HIS ONE AND ONLY BOOK.
AVAILABLE FOR THE FIRST TIME SINCE 1976

TO ORDER YOUR COPY
CALL 0845 143 0001
OR LOG ON TO WWW.MERSEYSHOP.COM

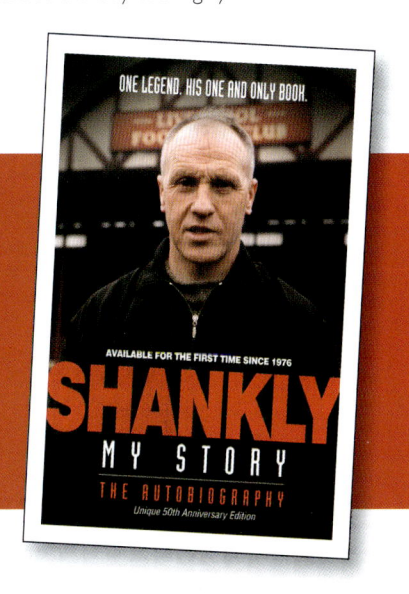

SHANKLY
MY STORY
THE AUTOBIOGRAPHY
Unique 50th Anniversary Edition

60

THE SWANSONG

Shankly watches a trial game towards the end of his spell as Liverpool manager

50 YEARS OF SHANKLY

Alone with his thoughts at
Wembley on the eve of the
1974 FA Cup final

The swansong

AFTER clinching the double of the league and UEFA Cup in 1972/73, the scene seemed to be set for another glorious period in Liverpool's history.

Little did Reds fans know it but their team's FA Cup success against Newcastle at the end of the 1973/74 season would mark the beginning of the end of Shankly's spell in charge.

There were few changes to the squad ahead of the new season as Shankly gave his backing to the men who had helped the club to that unprecedented double. One difference was the captain, with Emlyn Hughes succeeding Tommy Smith as the Reds' leader.

Despite a strong challenge, Leeds United won the race for the title with Liverpool having to content themselves with the runners-up berth.

But there was still silverware in May as the Reds won their second FA Cup. Their opponents at Wembley were Newcastle United, whose players made plenty of pre-match press predictions about what would happen beneath the Twin Towers.

Liverpool, however, were more than ready for them, playing some classy football in overcoming the Geordies 3-0 in a one-sided affair.

As the players paraded the cup, Reds fans were already turning their minds to what glories lay in store in 1975/76. Amid their celebrations, it seemed impossible that their team would have a new man in charge. But on July 12, Shankly shocked the football world to its very foundations by revealing his intention to stand down.

The reasons for his decision have never been fully explained. In his autobiography, Shankly said that he felt very tired at the end of that season and wanted the chance to re-charge his batteries and spend time doing other things.

In the years afterwards however there was a lingering sense that Shankly was trying too hard to justify his decision. Despite the brave face he always put on it, there is little doubt that he was never fully at ease after opting to call time on his spell in charge of the club he loved.

"I felt that the Liverpool people were my kind of people," he said in retirement. "What I achieved at Anfield I did for those fans. Together we turned Liverpool into one huge family, something alive and vibrant and warm and successful. I thank God for the people of Merseyside. The attitude of the people towards me and my family is stronger now than it ever was. I never cheated them and they've never let me down."

Legacies such as his can be a big burden to bear but no-one would have been more delighted than Shankly to see the club continue to build on the incredible platform he laid.

A complete one-off, Liverpool were lucky to have reaped the benefits of Shankly's infectious love for the game.

On the 50th anniversary of his arrival at Anfield, Liverpool fans have every reason to celebrate an incredible man who played such a pivotal part in the club's rich tapestry.

Liverpool celebrate after scoring their third goal against Newcastle United at Wembley

50 YEARS OF SHANKLY

64

Shankly joins a delighted Liverpool fan on the Wembley pitch

THE SWANSONG

Shankly is joined by a special passenger on the train home to Liverpool in May 1974: the FA Cup

Left: Saluting fans who came out in force to pay tribute to their heroes' open-top bus victory parade in the city

50 YEARS OF SHANKLY

A sad day as Shankly announces his retirement on July 12, 1974

THE SWANSONG

50 YEARS OF SHANKLY

One of Shankly's last acts as Liverpool manager was to announce the signing of Ray Kennedy from Arsenal

Carrying on until his successor was appointed, Shankly was back at Melwood for the team's return to training on July 15, 1974

THE SWANSONG

A last hurrah as Shankly leads out Liverpool for the FA Charity Shield

The Liverpool team Shankly handed over to Bob Paisley

Celebrating with the FA Charity Shield after Liverpool had defeated Leeds on penalties

Now then, young man... Shankly passes on some tips to Brian Clough

THE SWANSONG

An emotional Liverpol fan thanks
Shankly for the memories

50 YEARS OF SHANKLY

MAN OF THE PEOPLE

Switching on the Christmas
Lights in Liverpool city centre

Interviewing Prime Minister Harold Wilson
for a Radio City chat show in 1975

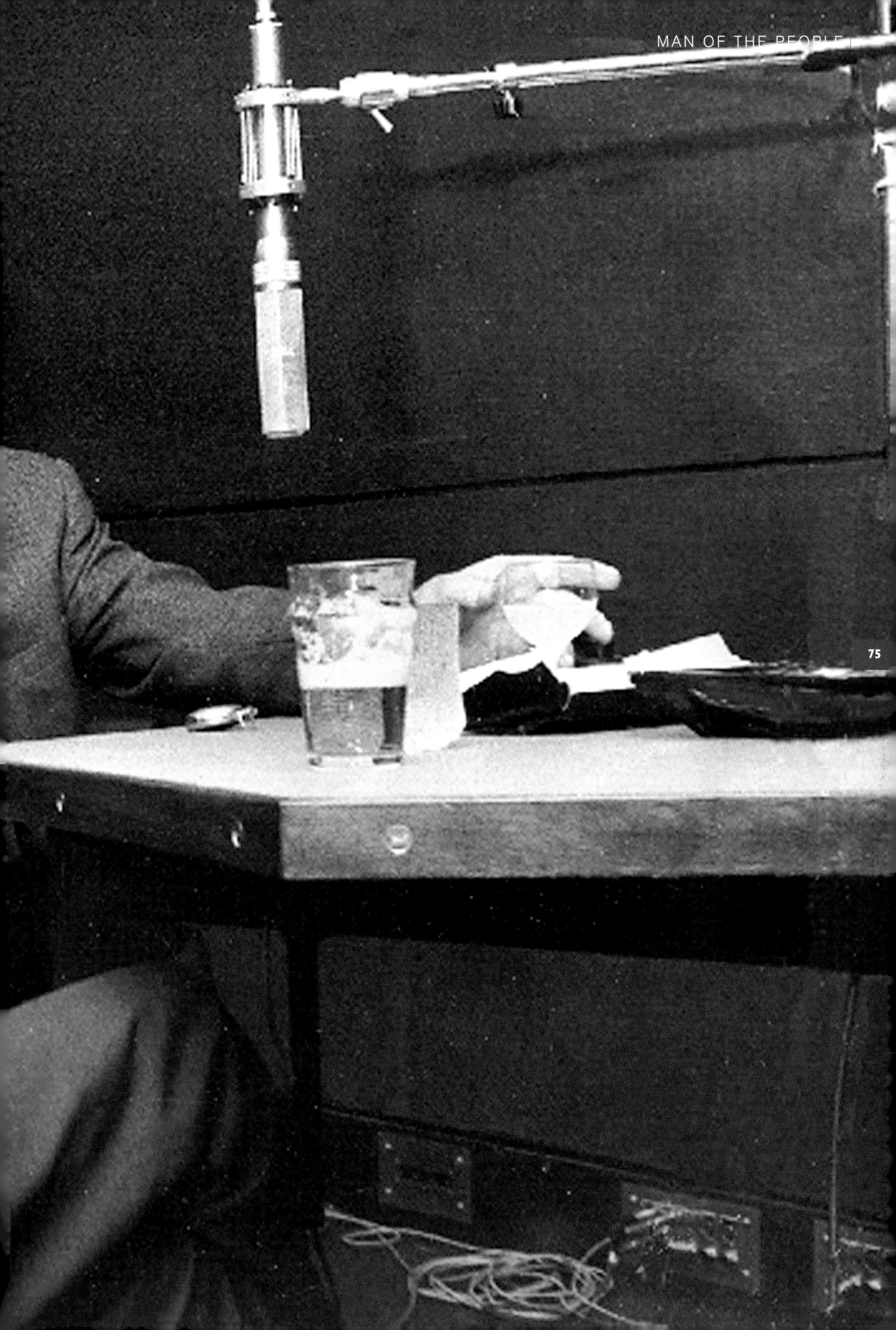

Proudly showing off his retirement card from The Kop, above, and, right, kissing his daughter on her wedding day

FAMILY LIFE

Showing off another award with wife Nessie, left, and below, spending time in the garden with the family

Bottom: With granddaughters Karen and Pauline

Right: When Shankly presented a sword of honour to European Footballer of the Year Kevin Keegan in 1979, the striker immediately handed it back and dedicated it to his former boss

Below: Launching a record with the help of Denis Law, who he managed at Huddersfield, and Emlyn Hughes

Bottom: With Grand National great Red Rum

OFF THE FIELD

The Shankly statue at Anfield and, left, The Kop pays homage during the celebrations to mark the the 40th anniversary of his arrival at Anfield

When FOOTBALL Was FOOTBALL

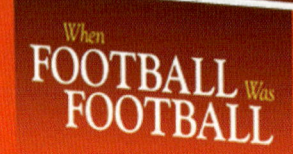

LIVERPOOL
A Nostalgic Look at a Century of the Club

OUT NOW £18.99 plus P&P
Call 01963 442030 & quote WF.

This is a unique and magnificent collection of photographs of Liverpool Football Club from the very early days until 1992.

www.MirrorFootball.co.uk
Available from all good bookshops or
ORDER DIRECT on Tel: 01963 442030

Books for enthusiasts by enthusiasts

Haynes

OBE

Shankly proudly shows off his OBE as he stands outside Buckingham Palace with wife Nessie following his investiture

"My idea was to build Liverpool into a bastion of invincibility. Napoleon had that idea. He wanted to conquer the bloody world. I wanted Liverpool to be untouchable. My idea was to build Liverpool up and up until eventually everyone would have to submit, give in"